B...
Sketch...

London Adam & Charles Black

1 London
2 Edinburgh
3 Cambridge
4 Stratford on Avon
5 Bath and Wells
6 Canterbury

PUBLISHED BY
A. & C. BLACK · SOHO SQUARE · LONDON W.

BATH AND

WELLS

A SKETCH-
BOOK BY
D.S. ANDREWS

A AND C. BLACK LTD.
SOHO SQ: LONDON.W.

DRAWINGS.

THE ROMAN BATH, BATH.

THE GUILDHALL & ABBEY. BATH.   D.S ANDREWS 1910.

HIGH ST. BATH. D.S.ANDREWS 1919

ST MICHAELS CHURCH, BATH.

D. S. ANDREWS

Pulteney Bridge. Bath.   BD ANDREWS

Pulteney Bridge, BATH, from Terrace.　　　　R S Andrews

NORTH PARADE BRIDGE. BATH.

D S ANDREWS 1914.

SOUTHGATE St, BATH.   D. S. ANDREWS 1919

MINERAL WATER FOUNTAIN. BATH.   D.S. ANDREWS. 1911

THE VICTORIA MEMORIAL, VICTORIA PARK, BATH.

DOOR, BEAU NASH'S HOUSE.   D.S.ANDREW'S '19

BATH FROM BEECHEN CLIFF.

D.S. ANDREWS. 1919.

D.S ANDREWS 1919.   BATH. from ALEXANDRA PARK

WELLS CATHEDRAL From South West   D.S ANDREW 1919

MARKET PLACE. WELLS.   D.SANDREWS. 1915

PALACE GATEWAY. WELLS.   D.S. ANDREWS. 1911.

WELLS·CATHEDRAL   D.S.ANDREWS.

FROM CENTRAL TOWER, of Cathedral, WELLS.   D S ANDREWS 1919

D.S.ANDREWS 1919.　　　CHAIN GATE. CCELLS

GATEHOUSE, VICARS CLOSE, WELLS.   D.S.ANDREWS

DOOR. VICAR'S CLOSE. WELLS.   D.S.ANDREWS.1919

D.S.ANDREWS 1919.   BISHOPS PALACE, WELLS.

WELLS CATHEDRAL from Top HILL.

First published in Great Britain in 1920
by A&C Black Publishers
36 Soho Square
London W1D 3QY
www.acblack.com

This edition published 2009

© 1920, 2009 A&C Black

ISBN 978-14081-1125-3

A CIP record of this book is available from the British Library

Printed and bound in China